Drips and Drops

Written by Sandeep Ghana

Illustrated by Juan Romero

Decodable Book

25

Initial and Final Consonant Blends

drips	splat
drops	trip
plans	

Consonant *Bb* /b/	**Consonant *Jj* /j/**
big	jam
bit	just
Ben	

High-Frequency Words

again	new	saw	was
be	our	there	were
could	over	they	

It was one.
We had plans to go over to see Ben.
He has a new pup.

We were to be at his home at two.

We saw the big drips and drops.
We just sat in our home.

Could we be there at three?
We were in a bit of a jam.
Could we be with Ben and the pup?

The drips and drops came again.
They went splat.

Our mom sat with us.

The trip was late.
We saw Ben and the pup at four.